AR Level: 4.3

Pts. 0.5

Lexile: 670b

The NFL's Greatest Teams

Oakland Raiders

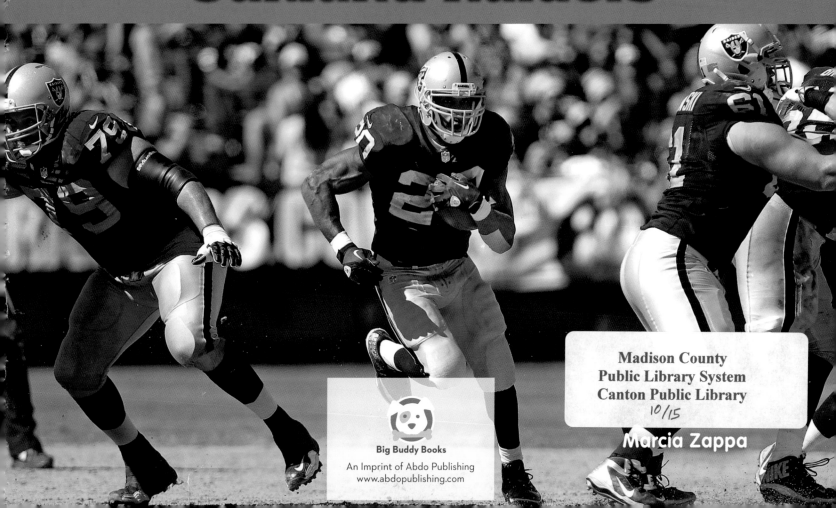

Big Buddy Books
An Imprint of Abdo Publishing
www.abdopublishing.com

Marcia Zappa

www.abdopublishing.com

Published by Abdo Publishing, a division of ABDO, PO Box 398166, Minneapolis, Minnesota 55439.
Copyright © 2015 by Abdo Consulting Group, Inc. International copyrights reserved in all countries. No part
of this book may be reproduced in any form without written permission from the publisher. Big Buddy Books™
is a trademark and logo of Abdo Publishing.

Printed in the United States of America, North Mankato, Minnesota.
092014
012015

THIS BOOK CONTAINS
RECYCLED MATERIALS

Cover Photo: ASSOCIATED PRESS.
Interior Photos: ASSOCIATED PRESS (pp. 5, 7, 8, 9, 14, 17, 18, 19, 20, 21, 23, 25, 28, 29); Getty Images
    (pp. 13, 17, 20, 27); Sports Illustrated/Getty Images (p. 11).

Coordinating Series Editor: Rochelle Baltzer
Contributing Editors: Bridget O'Brien, Sarah Tieck
Graphic Design: Michelle Labatt

Library of Congress Cataloging-in-Publication Data

Zappa, Marcia, 1985-
  Oakland Raiders / Marcia Zappa.
      pages cm. -- (The NFL's Greatest Teams)
  Audience: Age: 7-11.
  ISBN 978-1-62403-590-6
  1. Oakland Raiders (Football team)--History--Juvenile literature. I. Title.
  GV956.O24Z37 2015
  796.332'640979466--dc23
                          2014026443

Contents

A Winning Team

The Oakland Raiders are a team in the National Football League (NFL). They are based in Oakland, California. They have been a **professional** football team for more than 50 years.

The Raiders have had good seasons and bad. But time and again, they've proven themselves. Let's see what makes the Raiders one of the NFL's greatest teams.

Silver and black are the team's colors.

League Play

Team Standings

The AFC and the National Football Conference (NFC) make up the NFL. Each conference has a north, south, east, and west division.

The NFL got its start in 1920. Its teams have changed over the years. Today, there are 32 teams. They make up two conferences and eight divisions.

The Raiders play in the West Division of the American Football Conference (AFC). This division also includes the Denver Broncos, the Kansas City Chiefs, and the San Diego Chargers.

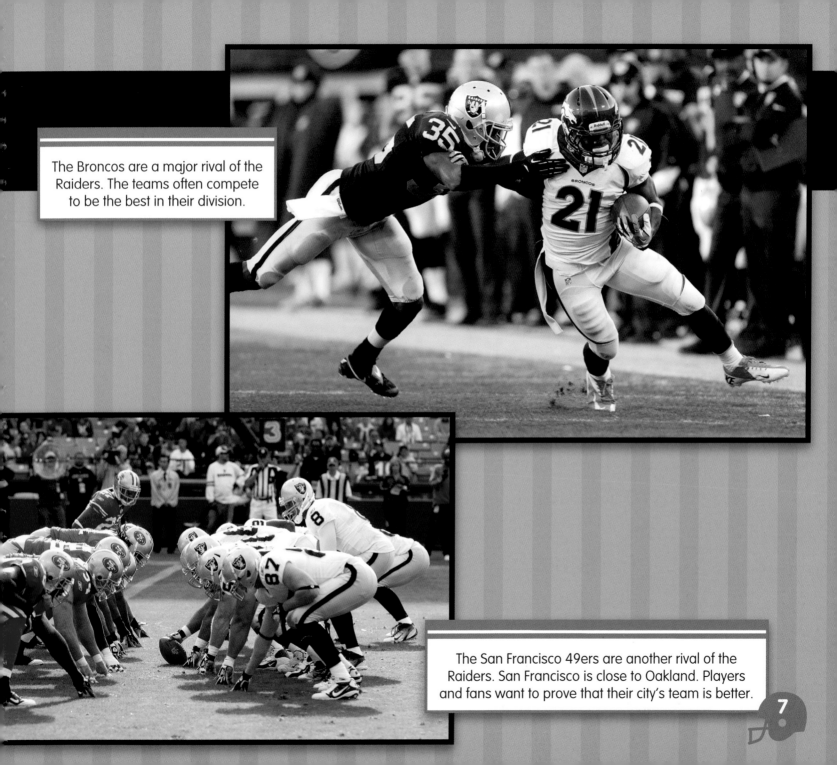

The Broncos are a major rival of the Raiders. The teams often compete to be the best in their division.

The San Francisco 49ers are another rival of the Raiders. San Francisco is close to Oakland. Players and fans want to prove that their city's team is better.

Kicking Off

The Raiders started out in 1960. They were one of the first teams in the American Football League (AFL). In 1970, the AFL joined the NFL.

Like many new teams, the Raiders struggled. In 1963, they hired Al Davis as head coach. He quickly turned the team around.

In time, Davis became the team's owner. In 2011, his son Mark (*right*) took over as owner.

No Home Field

Before 1966, the Raiders didn't have a home stadium. They played home games in San Francisco and at a temporary Oakland stadium.

Davis passed away in 2011. A flame at the team's home stadium honors his memory.

Highlight Reel

In 1963, the Raiders had their first winning season. In 1968, they played in their first Super Bowl. But, they lost to the Green Bay Packers.

In 1969, John Madden took over as head coach. He led the team to many winning seasons. In 1977, the Raiders made it back to the Super Bowl. This time, they won!

Win or Go Home

NFL teams play 16 regular season games each year. The teams with the best records are part of the play-off games. Play-off winners move on to the conference championships. Then, conference winners face off in the Super Bowl!

In the 1977 Super Bowl, the Raiders beat the Minnesota Vikings 32–14.

11

The Raiders continued their strong play. In 1981, they won another Super Bowl. Then in 1982, owner Al Davis moved the team to Los Angeles, California.

The Raiders did well in Los Angeles. They won their third Super Bowl in 1984. In 1995, Davis moved the team back to Oakland.

The Raiders struggled in Oakland. But in 2003, they made it back to the Super Bowl. This time, they lost. Today, they are trying to get back to their former glory.

Across the Years

The Raiders are the only NFL team to play in a Super Bowl during the 1960s, the 1970s, and the 1980s.

In 1981, the Raiders beat the Philadelphia Eagles in the Super Bowl (*below*). In 1984, they beat the Washington Redskins (*left*).

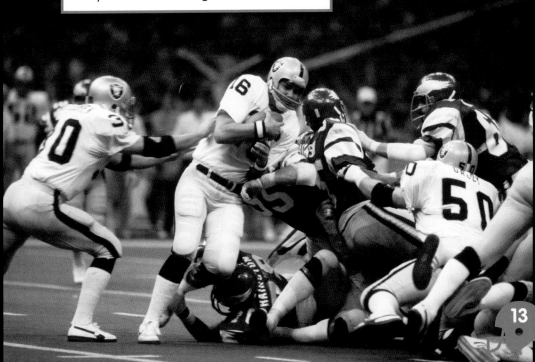

Halftime! Stat Break

Team Records

RUSHING YARDS
Career: Marcus Allen, 8,545 yards (1982–1992)
Single Season: Marcus Allen, 1,759 yards (1985)
PASSING YARDS
Career: Ken Stabler, 19,078 yards (1970–1979)
Single Season: Rich Gannon, 4,689 yards (2002)

RECEPTIONS
Career: Tim Brown, 1,070 receptions (1988–2003)
Single Season: Tim Brown, 104 receptions (1997)
ALL-TIME LEADING SCORER
Sebastian Janikowski, 1,489 points (2000–2013)

Fan Fun

NICKNAMES: The Silver and Black,
The Men in Black
STADIUM: O.co Coliseum
LOCATION: Oakland, California
MASCOT: Raider Rusher

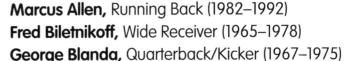

Pro Football Hall of Famers & Their Years with the Raiders

Marcus Allen, Running Back (1982–1992)
Fred Biletnikoff, Wide Receiver (1965–1978)
George Blanda, Quarterback/Kicker (1967–1975)
Willie Brown, Cornerback (1967–1978)
Dave Casper, Tight End (1974–1980, 1984)
Al Davis, Coach/Owner (1963–2011)
Ray Guy, Punter (1973–1986)
Mike Haynes, Cornerback (1983–1989)
Ted Hendricks, Linebacker (1975–1983)
Howie Long, Defensive End (1981–1993)
John Madden, Coach (1969–1978)
Jim Otto, Center (1960–1974)
Art Shell, Tackle (1968–1982)
Gene Upshaw, Guard (1967–1981)

Famous Coaches

Al Davis (1963–1965)
John Madden (1969–1978)

Championships

SUPER BOWL APPEARANCES:
1968, 1977, 1981, 1984, 2003

SUPER BOWL WINS:
1977, 1981, 1984

15

Coaches' Corner

John Madden started as an assistant coach for the Raiders in 1967. In 1969, he became the head coach.

Madden led the team for ten years. During that time, the Raiders never had a losing season. In 1977, Madden led them to their first Super Bowl win.

Dennis Allen became head coach of the Raiders in 2012.

In 1969, Madden was the youngest head coach in the NFL.

17

Star Players

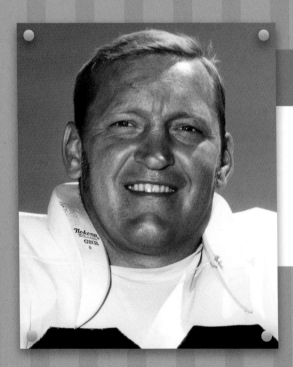

Jim Otto CENTER (1960–1974)

Jim Otto played for the Raiders his whole **career**. He was the starting center for 15 seasons. Otto helped the team reach its first Super Bowl. He played in all nine AFL All-Star games and the first three Pro Bowls, which is the NFL's all-star game.

Fred Biletnikoff WIDE RECEIVER (1965–1978)

Fred Biletnikoff helped the Raiders make it to the 1968 Super Bowl and win the 1977 Super Bowl. He was named the Most Valuable Player (MVP) of the 1977 game! When he **retired**, he had 589 receptions for 8,974 yards and 76 touchdowns. Those were team records at the time.

Willie Brown CORNERBACK (1967–1978)

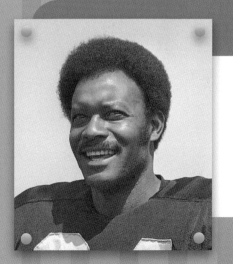

When Willie Brown joined the Raiders, he was already a star with the Denver Broncos. But, he played even better with the Raiders! He helped the team make it to two Super Bowls. Brown had 39 **interceptions** with the Raiders. That ties Lester Hayes for the team record.

Gene Upshaw GUARD (1967–1981)

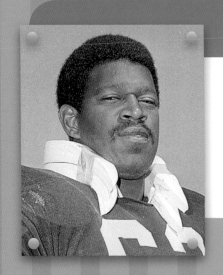

Gene Upshaw was the team's first choice in the 1967 **draft**. He became a starter right away. Upshaw was known for his size, strength, and leadership. He stayed with the Raiders his whole **career**. He played in 307 games, including three Super Bowls!

Art Shell TACKLE (1968–1982)

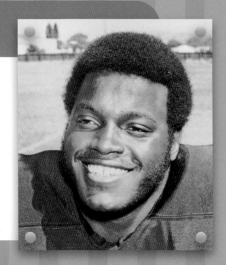

Art Shell became a starter during his third season. Soon, he was known as one of the best offensive linemen. He was skilled at guarding the quarterback and blocking for running plays. Shell helped the Raiders win the Super Bowl in 1977 and 1981. He played in the Pro Bowl eight times.

Marcus Allen RUNNING BACK (1982–1992)

Marcus Allen was the team's first pick in the 1982 **draft**. He was skilled at rushing and catching passes. In 1984, he helped the team win the Super Bowl and was named its MVP. In 1985, Allen rushed for 1,759 yards and had 67 receptions for 555 yards. He was named the NFL's MVP!

Tim Brown WIDE RECEIVER (1988–2003)

Tim Brown played for the Raiders for 16 seasons. He was a punt returner and wide receiver. Brown helped the team make it to the 2003 Super Bowl. During his **career**, Brown caught 1,070 receptions for 14,934 yards. That is more than any other Raider.

O.co Coliseum

The Raiders play home games at O.co Coliseum in Oakland. It opened in 1966. It can hold about 63,000 people. The Oakland Athletics baseball team also plays home games there.

O.co Coliseum was first called Oakland-Alameda County Coliseum. Most fans still refer to it by this name.

Name Game

O.co is short for the online store Overstock.com. It is said "oh-dot-koh."

Go Silver and Black!

Thousands of fans flock to the team's stadium to see the Raiders play home games. Some call their team the "Silver and Black" or the "Men in Black."

In 2013, the Raiders got a new **mascot**. Raider Rusher is based on a cartoon called *NFL Rush Zone*. He appears at home games to meet the team's young fans.

O.co Coliseum has a section called the Black Hole. Fans that sit there cheer loudly and wear wild silver and black outfits!

BLACK HOLE® AL

25

Final Call

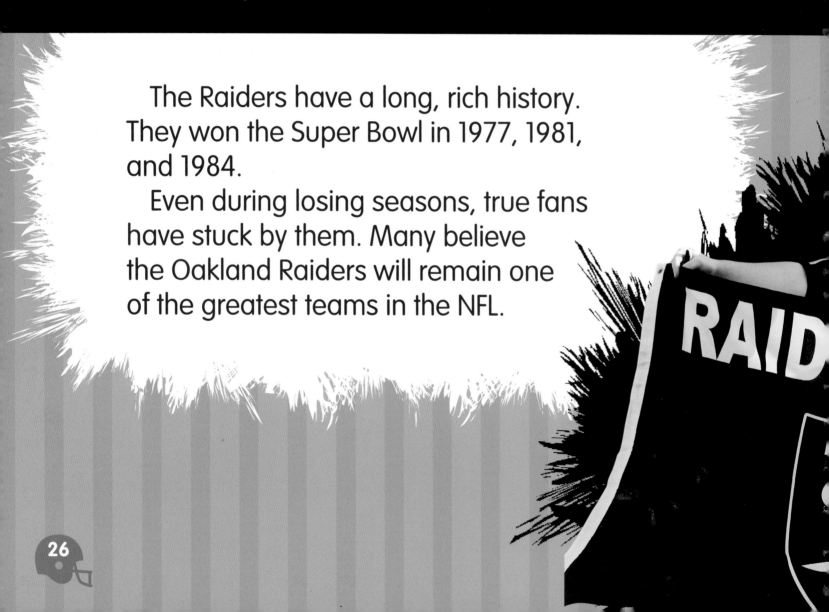

The Raiders have a long, rich history. They won the Super Bowl in 1977, 1981, and 1984.

Even during losing seasons, true fans have stuck by them. Many believe the Oakland Raiders will remain one of the greatest teams in the NFL.

Raiders fans are called the Raider Nation.

Through the Years

1960
The Oakland Raiders become an AFL team.

1963
The team has its first winning season.

1968
The Raiders play in their first Super Bowl. They lose to the Green Bay Packers 33–14.

1970
The AFL joins the NFL.

1977
The Raiders get their first Super Bowl win! They beat the Minnesota Vikings 32–14.

2011

Longtime owner Al Davis passes away. His son Mark becomes the team's new owner.

2003

The team plays in its fifth Super Bowl.

1995

The Raiders return to Oakland.

1978

After ten straight winning seasons, John Madden **retires** from coaching.

1982

Owner Al Davis moves the Raiders to Los Angeles.

1980

Jim Otto becomes the first Raider in the Pro Football Hall of Fame.

Postgame Recap

1. How many losing seasons did the Raiders have during John Madden's ten seasons as head coach?
   A. 0   **B**. 1   **C**. 9

2. What is the name of the stadium where the Raiders play home games?
   A. Oakland Coliseum
   B. Raiders Coliseum
   C. O.co Coliseum

3. Name 3 of the 14 Raiders in the Pro Football Hall of Fame.

4. Why are the 49ers a rival of the Raiders?
   A. These teams often compete to be the best in their division.
   B. San Francisco is near Oakland and players and fans want to prove their city's team is better.
   C. They have stolen star players and coaches from them.

Glossary

career a period of time spent in a certain job.

draft a system for professional sports teams to choose new players. When a team drafts a player, they choose that player for their team.

interception (ihn-tuhr-SEHP-shuhn) when a player catches a pass that was meant for the other team's player.

mascot something to bring good luck and help cheer on a team.

professional (pruh-FEHSH-nuhl) paid to do a sport or activity.

retire to give up one's job.

Websites

To learn more about the NFL's Greatest Teams, visit **booklinks.abdopublishing.com**. These links are routinely monitored and updated to provide the most current information available.

Index